SUSURROS

A

MI

PADRE

ERICK SÁENZ

the operating system c. 2018

the operating system print//document

SUSURROS A MI PADRE

ISBN: 978-1-946031-25-9
Library of Congress Control Number: 2018943325
copyright © 2018 by Erick Sáenz
edited and designed by Lynne DeSilva-Johnson

For additional questions regarding reproduction, quotation, or to request a pdf for review contact **operator@theoperatingsystem.org**

This text was set in Minion, Franchise, and OCR-A Standard.

Books from The Operating System are distributed to the trade by SPD/Small Press Distribution, with ePub and POD via Ingram, with production by Spencer Printing, in Honesdale, PA, in the USA.

The operating system is a member of the Radical Open Access Collective, a community of scholar-led, not-for-profit presses, journals and other open access projects. Now consisting of 40 members, we promote a progressive vision for open publishing in the humanities and social sciences.
Learn more at: http://radicaloa.disruptivemedia.org.uk/about/

Your donation makes our publications, platform and programs possible! We <3 You.
bit.ly/growtheoperatingsystem

the operating system

141 Spencer Street #203
Brooklyn, NY 11205
www.theoperatingsystem.org
operator@theoperatingsystem.org

SUSURROS

A

MI

PADRE

ERICK
SÁENZ

A B C **CH** D E F G H I
J K L **LL** M N **Ñ** O P Q
R **RR** S T U V W X Y Z

> *"They call me in words of another language. My brown body searches the streets for the dye that will color my thoughts"*
>
> Lorna Dee Cervantes

For my mother who tirelessly played the role of both parents

[PROCESS]

My relationship with Mexico began early on, day trips across the
border. The treks blur together. What does stand out:
// Bottles of Sidral from Woolworths
// Sickness from coarse roads
// Packets of chicklets at the border
// The expanse of ocean and the hem that represented the other side

We were all birthed. My father, no exception. He came from Durango. I've never been there, need to google a map of Mexico. I stare at it for a long time trying to locate the city, a red dot just to right of dead center. I realize later the state is much larger than this dot I associate with his birthplace.

He didn't talk much about growing up, and to be honest, I never asked him. Our relationship was not the kind for casual conversation. Talks usually occurred late at night, when we were both in altered states (me from sleep, him from drink). Or Saturday afternoons in front of the television where soccer filled the silence.

According to maps it's a 5 hour//46 minute drive from Durango to Monterrey. I meditate on whether or not he ever saw a large body of water before arriving in Texas. What is it like growing up landlocked?

, 2014 … I lose track of the years as I grow older, but at some point I tire of living in the sprawl of Southern California and move back to a college town 6 hours north. I call it a "reset." I abandon concrete/heat and am rebirthed in thick fog.
This is the beginning of my reconnection;
//long stretch of highway
//"corridos" through the night
//opportunity to form the words I thought lost
//cool wind pushing me forward

[CREATING A NARRATIVE]

There was Raul, Roberto, Rosa, Concepcion, Rudy, Rafael, Esthela, Rosalinda, Rene, and Ricardo. Siblings sharing sparse living conditions, Tiny brown bodies piled into single beds.

I know them in one way or another. They all had something, distinctions:
bolo tie, scarred face, temper, jesus, alcohol.

I never met my grandmother who everyone called "Chauqita." I ask my mother what it was short for, assume a nickname of sorts. Her name was Isaura. I look at pictures when I return to Los Angeles. She gleams in that authentic way that we all attempt via countless filters on social media. A hardness peers through, similar to that which my father carried.

My grandfather was a mystery, although I did know him: stern faced and dressed as if he were going for a fancy dinner, cream colored recliner, parrot on shoulder. I was afraid of the parrot, although often coaxed to feed it sunflower seeds. He gave out $5 bills. This was our relationship.

[SIBLING INPUT]

I reach the point where I want to know if it's only me who lost his language somewhere along the way. I decide to email my sister and brother, find out how it was before I became of this world. This isn't just about me anymore, it's about family history & language. What I collect:

// Spanish was sacred for tios/as, at home for secrets
// The neighborhood before I arrived was brown
// Both siblings still practice, but feel loss
// My siblings' loss does not correlate to my own

[PROCESS]

November 5th, 2015 … my aunt in Los Angeles whose house I knew well posts a picture of grandparents and children. Some remarks:
// 7 familiar faces
// 6 smiles
// 5 frowns

November 11th, 2015 … I track down my godfather's daughter on social media. Although younger, we were close as children. She is the only connection I still have to Monterrey. Her last memory of me; 10 years old and lost on the beach in Corpus Christi, Texas.

//MEMORIAS

CHRIST THE KING ROMAN CATHOLIC CHURCH

[stand]

Towering right off Melrose, the thick of Mexican immigrants.
A few blocks away güeros: espresso shots, vintage clothes. The
hollywood dream.

*

Remember the pews;
smooth to touch.

Remember the hymn books; stale & worn.

Remember the kneelers;
ragged // crimson

*

Tia Concha's was close, two blocks south. I'd enjoy the stroll, sticky
pan dulce. The clicking of dress shoes on concrete. "Buenos dias"
echoing down the avenue.

*

The sun and heat were unrelenting. I'd lose myself in the
illuminated stained glass and shiny streams of dust, painted rose.

[sit]

I never knew if I really believed, mostly people watched as
everyone around me lowered their eyes and recited in whispers.
I was absent in the words. Nearby St. Faustina's look, damning.

*

After, we'd all congregate in front, the "peace be with you" turned to gossip. He'd be standing there watching, crown and all.

*

Years later, I still smell those books and see the floating dust. Still wavering.

[repeat]

FATHERLAND

*

3 day-haze in the back of an '89 Chevy Suburban. Nestled between luggage: Gameboy on my lap, road unfolding around me.

*

Monterrey was his home, seemed at ease amongst the grey industry. I'd never considered the idea of being from somewhere, no distinction between here and there.

*

One year, it snowed. 12 year old me in hideous kelly green sweats & brown leather jacket, background scrubbed; transparent.
Not pictured: Father with camera, roaring directions.

*

Some relatives would dote on me endlessly, try their best English. Others would refuse, speak in that regional way: all tongue like the Spaniards. As if the fog stuffed their mouths.

*

My cousins there too, gathered arm-to-arm, pool cues in tow. We all spoke English, our first language slowly disappearing.
Not pictured: father, boisterous in the living room from drink.

Padriño's ranch; my 10th birthday w/ a beaten piñata & face covered in frosting. I cried endlessly, unaware of the tradition that was not practiced at home. Humiliation was nothing new, cut deeper in another dialect.

*

My aunt had the nickname Mother Teresa, would guilt us into church. Spanish mass, lost on American ears. I pretended to believe, fantasized about divine intervention.

*

I haven't been back since. I imagine everything the same without me; buildings, ash canvas, mountain backdrop. My aunt attending church. That ominous ranch.
Not pictured: The Saenz youth, now men. Father's remains, clumps in the Pacific.

IDIOMAS

*

An early memory: one hand clasps a bowl of soup. The other extends, fingers out. Cuchara off my lips seamlessly. Jack and Jill Preschool. 1983.

*

I try researching the school online. Like my native tongue, the site no longer exists. Memory // dream. What severs the two?

*

I text my mother: "why was I put into an all-English speaking Kindergarten?"

A full minute of ghostly ellipses.

*

It only took months to become proficient. One language fell behind the other.

*

Finally, my phone buzzes: "no bilingual allowed at the time."

*

My partner sends me a pdf, "brief history of bilingual education." I learn that full assimilation usually happens after three generations.

*

I'm the first generation born here on both sides of my family.

*

What I learn: shortly after I was born my parents left West Whittier for the East side. My mother uses barrio, her choice of noun ominous.

*

What I learn: my sister was being recruited by a local gang. White suburbia distanced us.

*

Returning home, I attempt to visit the preschool. Now a church, its spires cast shadows on trimmed lawn.

GIANT-ASS LÍQUIDO

*

I add an accent to my last name in college, a mark of pride. A mark of something.

*

I speak Spanish fluidly at the panaderia. The woman responds politely, looks amused. My assumed whiteness makes me stick out amongst the pan dulce racks. I take pleasure in rolling my "r's."

*

When he passed, so did my language. Gone were the weekly trips to Tía Concha's, the one who refused to speak English to me. I had to practice, out of necessity. Our routine: ask; correct and try again.

*

I was overly excited when someone signed my yearbook in Spanish. Read the text over and over, felt the words smooth and glossy. I wanted to go back and respond, prove to him I could. As if it weren't history.

*

At home it was mostly English, the other language reserved for anger. I knew all the bad words first.

*

"What would you like?"

"Me das un líquido de piña," I say with a certain cockiness I can't explain. I know she speaks English. *I can order in our native tongue. Don't worry.*

[PROCESS]

April 3rd, 2016 …On a typically warm afternoon in Los Angeles my partner and I visit the family church where everyone was "married and buried." Everything looked just as I left it so many years before.

August 25th, 2016… my partner and I visit the grave site of infamous San Jose "robin hood" Tiburcio Vasquez. I take a video of a torn Mexican flag flapping in the wind with the caption *for my father who, if nothing else, gave me a culture I love and appreciate #sentimientos.*

December 28th, 2016 … My partner gifts me a family ancestry kit that requires spitting into a tube for several minutes. What's already known: I'm equal parts German & Mexican. I feel nervous about the unknown.

//GÜERO

In 11th grade I attempt to join MECHA. Whether or not imagined, I feel pairs of eyes and mouths agape when I show up to the meeting during lunch hour. I turn around and let them burn into the back of my head. I never return.

I have a friend in 7th grade who speaks only Spanish. We communicate in broken languages, filling in gaps with the comfortable one. At the end of the year he writes in my yearbook. All summer I sit and marvel at the words, feel ink on finger tips. I only understand bits, need my mother to help translate the whole message. I feel an odd love for these words.

I take Spanish as my foreign language in 9th grade. The first thing that happens is the teacher assigns me a different name, more suitable to Spanish. In a single stroke I'm erased and reborn as "Enrique." More evidence that I am not Mexican enough.

//CON VERGÜENZA

...when I show the 1947 movie adaptation of "The Pearl" in my class. Mexican director Emilio Fernández does not shy away from the underlying political message of anti-colonialism in his version. It's there in the beautiful choreographed dancing, my people's music familiar yet distant. It's there in Kino's disdain towards his oppressors. My student fidgets, looks lost. I struggle with the impulse to explain what's happening, talk over the *baile folklorico.* "They're just walking around," he says.

I bite my lip and feel my face go flush...

...when I have to translate for my white co-workers at the continuation school in Salinas. They speak little Spanish, just enough to pass it on to someone else. I tense up whenever the phone rings, when *"uhn mo-men-to"* echoes in the halls. My body stiffens when parents wander in, questions that beg complicated answers. The process is tedious... //understand what the parent is saying // figure out how to answer // translate to spanish // speak it back. Mostly the words tumble out, their reactions speak loudly.

I bite my lip and feel my face go flush...

//CON ORGULLO

...at the *pulga*. I smile big as the sun slowly melts my *raspado* into liquid and then into nothing.

...at the *panaderia*. I smile big amidst the colorful breads, opaque metal sheets.

[PROCESS]

January 27th 2017 … I text my mother about pictures for the cover of the book you now hold. *Send me some where we are both happy*, I say. She only emails one of us together, and another of bb me in white polo shirt with my childhood home in the background.

January 30th, 2017 … I stand in front of a table of zinesters at a coffee shop and give an impromptu reading. I'm nervous, unsure how to begin explaining the project. I decide to read the "con verguenza" parts. It's odd hearing my words leave my throat, bounce off the walls.

February 19th, 2017 … I receive a letter from my mother that includes a family tree. It lists births and deaths, marriages, spawn, etc. It is confusing but using picture as reference I connect the dots, make sense of the scribbles.

February 25th 2017… this project is becoming larger, feel like I'm chasing the ghost of my father. The strange thing is there is no headstone to visit, ask questions, meditate on. How do you interrogate ashes lost at sea?

[CROSSINGS]

In 1956 my grandparents and 6 of 10 children packed up and got onto a train from Monterrey, Mexico to Laredo, Texas. They crossed over the Rio Grande, natural barrier between two countries. Details are missing of their trek across the landscapes of Texas, New Mexico, and Arizona. I only know the lengthy trip ended at Union Station, Los Angeles.

My father entered 4th grade.
He worked after school selling newspapers in the street.
He was saving to buy a bicycle.

He also experienced his first taste of racism: A friend banned from hanging around "those Mexicans." This is not the Los Angeles I know, flourishing Latinx community obvious via murals, street names, and shops throughout the city. I wonder what other acts of racism he faced. I wonder if these slowly wore him down, toughening the skin.

They would stay in the United States for a year before my grandmother decided she did not like the U.S. I press my mother and she discloses that family dynamics were strained, the house too crowded. I suspect she never fully assimilated, didn't want to.

Later my mother divulges that my grandmother was darker skinned than her in laws, "less than."

4 went back to Mexico, including my father. He was 5000 newspapers short of affording the bike.

[CROSSINGS]

I google bus routes between the cities. It is a 40-some hour journey spanning two countries. The routes: crossing into Texas and looping through the surreal deserts of the Southwest, or circling back through Mexico to Baja California, surfacing in sunlit San Diego.

When I was young, we had one route: a 3 day trek to San Antonio, and then a 5 hour trip south into Nuevo Leon. I still remember scenes from the trips...
// "world's tallest thermometer" in Baker
// towering cacti in Phoenix
// turquoise stands lining highway in New Mexico
// the ample flatness of Texas
// relentless current of the Rio Grande

[CROSSINGS]

What constitutes a boundary?

Online I find a history of the Rio Grande as natural demarcation. I learn that since 1848 the river has been acknowledged as a boundary between Mexico and the United States.

On the American side it is referred to as "grand river." On the Mexican side, another translation: "furious river."

It's difficult to not find the irony in these interpretations
One, revered protector
the other, obstacle to overcome

[CROSSINGS]

He made the trip again in 1963, almost 18 years old, this time by bus. He enrolled in adult school to improve English.
He washed dishes in a restaurant for a living.

My mother tells me he had a layover in an unknown town somewhere along the way. She says he decided to go to the movies to kill time, and nearly missed the bus, having to chase it down the highway.

… Image: father chasing after the vehicle, tie flapping, suitcase in tow.

Our relationship was light hearted in rare instances. I relish this image, although it is not from memory. How connected can I become to him through 3rd hand accounts?

… Image: father chasing vehicle, cursing loudly in the dust-up of tires.

[CROSSINGS]

He would spend the remaining years of his life in Southern California.
He met my mother.
They married.

Shortly after, my sister: first born.
4 years later: a son.
I came 9 years after that: a footnote to tense marriage.

He worked long nights in a car manufacturer warehouse.
To cope he'd fall into drinking binges, long nights and weekends.

This is the version of my father I knew best.

[CROSSINGS]

He passed in 2001 at the age of 55 from pulmonary fibrosis: a scarring of the lungs.

1. Imagine a topography map, unfolded
2. Sweep your hand across the surface, note contrast of smooth and rough

It is unknown whether or not that dusty warehouse did him in, the alcohol, or something else. In fact, in most cases doctors are unable to pinpoint exactly what causes the disease.

The most lucid effect is shortness of breath. My father used a breathing machine for the last years, an ominous hum lining the house every second.

His life ended at home, a quiet moment between my parents. I was off somewhere, unaware that the lost words I spoke before leaving would be our last.

No peace was made before he passed over into the unknown. But in a sense, the words in this book are enough.

[CROSSINGS]

My hours at work are reduced, and I spend a Friday morning listening to Unwound and meditating on barriers, both physical and not. Some are built, some assumed. If enough people believe, do they exist?

I keep going back to my father and the blatant racism he faced at 10 years old. How that must have bruised his brown body. How it might have prompted him to begin erasing his own origin. And in turn, urging us to erase ours.

My first language has faced a boundary since I began to forget it. Symptom of adapting language and/or lack of practice.

But I know this is imaginary too. My language slowly comes back every day.

[CROSSINGS]

I type this without receiving his input, a life relayed 3rd-hand via texts and emails.

I go to the library and find a series of records titled "Mexican - Texas Border Music". When I go home, I sit in the living room alone, dusk stealing through the windows, concentrating on the words...

Este es mi elogia, papi

//CORRIDO DE MONTERREY

My fondest memory of visiting Monterrey is not the family time. It is the mountain looming over the city. Dream-like, it rests in the back of my mind. What makes a memory? I go to the library and search "Monterrey, Mexico." I discover a CD by Oscar Chavez titled 'Puro Nuevo Leon.' The first track is titled *Corrido de Monterrey*, and describes the mountain I remember as a child. Memory confirmed.

I discover from the internet that the mountain is called *El Cerro de la Silla*, or Saddle Hill. I learn that it watches over the city at 5, 970 feet. From its peak, climbers have a panoramic view of metropolitan Monterrey and the nearby city of Guadalupe. I'm reminded of how permanent it felt, standing watch.

I remember how gray the city seemed, can't distinguish between commerce and winter bleakness. Everything felt hardened, unforgiving. I learn that Monterrey is a city of industry, the tech center of Mexico. It is well known for its strong business climate and institutions of higher education. This was not the lush, waterfront Mexico I had known before. Felt more like another Los Angeles.

//HISTORIAS: A.D.

They slowly fell off, one by one.
Was it difficult to face us, his *other* family?

I'd rather think that it was mutual.
My life was just beginning, 21 and free.

I mourned, sure. What I haven't forgotten...

Soft hum of machine

Anxious nights

Relief

———————————————

//HISTORIAS: B.D.

We'd alternate weekends. Tia Concha's off Melrose. Tia Carmen's off Wilshire. I'd swap languages; play with cousins, joke with uncles. On the drive home my father would be drunk, singing along to KEARTH. All those oldies I still know by heart.

Our relationship was fragile: words spoken softly when sober and angrily when drunk.

[PROCESS]

March 1st, 2017 … I receive an email that my test results are ready. I'm told to "log in and explore your ancestry composition." The highest percentage is Eastern European, followed by Native American. This makes me question the Latinx label I placed on myself. "Can I still claim my browness?"

March 12th, 2017 … My partner and I drive to a park on the East Side, in a neighborhood that she jokes is *rough* which is to say *brown*. It is a celebration: Aztec New Year. Roosters *ki-kiri-ki* in the background. Color ubiquitous, teeming over green. Over a hissing loudspeaker I hear, first shrill shrieks over rhythmic drums, and then an affirmation: "I don't care where you come from, we're all Mexican." I smile big and savor the agua fresca in my fist.

March 17th, 2017 … During a prep period I type *Durango, Mexico* into a search engine. I learn a local legend about the "death cell:" a man released from prison for capturing a colossal scorpion that was offing prisoners. I recall an identical beast, magnified by glass encasement, that rested atop the coffee table. I'd stare for hours, touch the smooth glass, imagine tiny movements.

March 18th, 2017 … I begin the process of adding the expansions to the full manuscript.
I text my mother:
"I'm almost done with this manuscript // I think // 42 pages // whew."
Her response:
"Love to read it all // thumbs up // smiley emoji."

March 28th, 2017 ... The arrival of spring prompts my partner to make boca burgers for dinner with a side of *pepinos con limon y tajin*. I'm reminded of saturday afternoons in my childhood home. Of Liga MX on the television. Of my father drinking beer to nurse a hangover. Of me happy to be spending time with him without anger.

//SUEÑOS

As a child I have a recurring dream: I'm walking home from school up the driveway of my childhood home. Two men are getting out of a truck. They stop to look at me.

I panic.

After his death, he appeared faceless. But I know it's him, feel all my inadequacies. Even after he couldn't physically haunt me, he still haunted me the same.

I hear him, familiar anger. I'm walking down the hallway of my childhood home. It is endless. I keep walking towards the voice.

I have one positive dream after his death: He says he's proud of me.

I don't respond.

SEMILLAS DE TAMARINDO

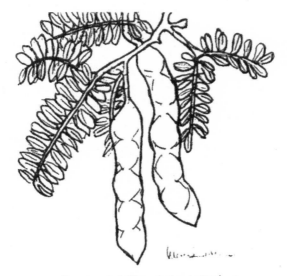

The tamarind (Tamarindus indica), a
leguminous fruit tree whose brown pods
contain an acid pulp used in cooking
and to prepare refreshing drinks. (½)

"Give up a tongue to take another, and so now I write in English"
--Angel Dominguez

Before bingo, there was loteria.

Every family has their own tradition. In my house, it was tamarindo seeds: endlessly greasy, that sweet salty taste. Handfuls falling slowly through my fingers.

I was losing my first language, Spanish tongue I still chase today. The words were easy to recite, pictures lending to understanding. I'd add traits to the pictures, create stories.

Strange how a child's game can hold such memories as these.

#40
...EL ALACRÁN...

SCORPION: STEALTH. EVIL.

Other associations:
// Coyotito's sting and the ensuing darkness in "The Pearl"
// Glass encased arachnid on display in childhood living room
// Symbol of Durango, my father's native land.

In Durango, Mexico there is folklore around a jail cell that contained a giant scorpion. Legend was that anyone who entered the space would immediately be devoured by this overgrown arachnid. Until finally, someone defeated him and was set free immediately for doing so.

This is my heritage.

CACTUS: HOLDER OF WATER. BEARER OF FRUIT.

Other associations:
// The endless temptation to press hand to spine
// Mother's ensalada de nopales: canned cactus, onion, tomato, chiles, oregano
// Life-like shapes in vast darkness

It took 3 days, through the vast emptiness of the southwest. Cacti for miles: towering in the day's sun, silent in the black night.

This is mother's dish, heavy with oregano.

DRUNK: FALSE PRIDE. FRIENDLY VIOLENCE.

Other associations:
// Father's problem with drink
// Backyard parties in high school
// Straight edge

Most weekends I would expect to be woken in the middle of the night, forced into conversations. Those talks we never had otherwise.

This is my rejection of the family disease.

BOTTLE: VESSEL. REFRESHMENT.

Other associations:
// Woolworth's
// Mundet Sidral
// Makeshift vase

We'd stop there every trip, my father searching for leather goods: boots, belts, etc. I liked the soda fountain, the countless varieties.

This is trips to Mexico.

#16
...LA BANDERA...

FLAG: EL TRI. HOPE, PURITY, BLOOD.

Other associations:
// Father's land
// Crystal water
// Surfing lessons

...After a while I stopped paddling, distracted by the streaks of red and endless blue. I sat out there until nightfall, watching.

This is the land from which my father came.

#14
...LA MUERTE...

DEATH: SELF-EXPLANATORY.

Other associations:
// Waiting
// My family's keeper
// Sickle & Scythe

Church off Melrose, where everyone was married or buried.

This is my family's legacy.

#24
...EL COTORRO...

PARROT: SPEAKER. FRIEND.

Other Associations:
// My grandfather's pet
// Sunflower seeds
// Tongue like iron (metaphor?)

Abuelo would sit in a dusty yellow recliner with fringes, pass out bills.

This is my grandfather's memory.

#46
...EL SOL...

SUN: LIGHTBEARER. HEAT.

Other associations:
// My first summer in Sacramento
// Water balloon fights
// Neighbor's pool

We'd play a game, who could stand the longest barefoot in the street.

This is summers in L.A.

#34
...EL SOLDADO...

SOLDIER: COURAGE. HONOR.

Other associations:
// G.I. Joes in the backyard
// Rubber band guns
// Desert Storm

His backyard led out to an alley: concrete and ivy. We'd play there for hours, playing war under a hot sun.

This is the last summer of innocence (7th grade).

#23
...LA LUNA...

MOON: BRIGHT. EVER-PRESENT.

Other associations:
//Pacific Ocean
// Long drives
// Father's worst

I'd take her there to sit on swings, stare at the endless black of sea. Romance hung thick.

These are my first attempts at love.

ROSE: FRAGRANT. FRAGILE

Other associations:
// Naglee & Dana
// Early love
// Gift for mother

My mother would water in the evenings, explaining that was the best time for flowers to feed. I'd be watching television, soothed by the sound of water splashing between soil and concrete.

This is the memory of my childhood home.

UMBRELLA: PROTECTOR. HIDER.

Other associations:
// First winter in Sacramento
// Smell of wet pavement
// Squeeks on classroom floor

After eating I immediately feel the need to wash my hands, regardless of what type of food it is or where I am.

This is my compulsive disorder.

I haven't played much since those days when the morning sunlight crept into my childhood home. Perhaps that makes it a child's game.

I see boards for sale at the *pulga*, clear bags with those familiar colorful pictures. I wonder if the different cards mean something more to others, too.

Or if these are my unique memories, transferred to a game, forever tied to family history.

GRAVE OF MY TIA CONCHA, 2018

(ORIGINALLY SCRAWLED ON GRAVE SITE, FORTHCOMING
VIA ELDERLY MAGAZINE IN COLLECTION TITLED *NORMALCIES*)

I started feeling it on the drive:
this wasn't supposed to be a
good time.

Tía Concha first.
It was hard to find,
a man helped me.
We spoke
Spanish.

We walked. He calmed me, made me feel at ease.

She passed in 2015
before that: a home.
Onset of Alzheimer's
disease my family knows well.

I got my hands in the earth, placed flowers in
mud.

Whispered in Spanish 'I love you,'

echoed words on gravestone:
"siempre vivirán en nuestros corazones."

TIA CARMEN AND I,
MARCH 2018

PATERNAL GRANDPARENTS WITH THEIR 8 CHILDREN. MY FATHER, 2ND TO LEFT
LOOKING OFF INTO DISTANCE UNSMILING, PERHAPS BORED.

CHILDHOOD HOME AS IT APPEARS TODAY. WHAT'S MISSING: BROWN/YELLOW GARAGE DOOR, JACARANDA TREE WHOSE STICKY PURPLE FLOWERS I HAD TO ENDLESSLY RAKE UP IN THE SUMMERS.

TORN MEXICAN FLAG UPON TIBURCIO VASQUEZ' GRAVE IN SAN JOSE, CA. MY PARTNER WOULD OFTEN VISIT THE GRAVESITE AND MEDITATE ON THE HISTORY OF SAN JOSE IN RELATION TO HER FAMILY'S HISTORY AND IN TURN, HER OWN. I WRITE ABOUT THIS VISIT IN THE MANUSCRIPT, BEING STRUCK BY THE IMAGERY OF THE WAVING FLAG, TORN BUT RESILIENT IN THE WIND.

CHRIST THE KING ROMAN CATHOLIC CHURCH, LOS ANGELES. ENDLESS FAMILY CEREMONIES: BIRTHS AND DEATHS. I VISITED FOR THE FIRST TIME IN A LONG WHILE IN 2016, AND WROTE ABOUT IT IN THE MANUSCRIPT.

IN TRANSLATION [IN TRANSLATION]

Dolores Dorantes was the first author I discovered who wrote in both English and Spanish, almost a conversation with herself in two languages. This quote in particular really empowered me to keep pushing through the material although at times it was difficult to face the past.

I found Dolores Dorantes by suggestion. Early in our relationship my partner and I traded books. One of the books I received was "Intervenir/Intervene," a book co-written with Rodrigo Flores Sanchez and translated by Jen Hofer. I was intimidated by the book; poetry *and* in translation.

"A music of evil persons,
a country with its back turned,

OPEN ME

the pit

CAST ME OUT

in this bedroom

I'M COLD"

At times the text is in conversation. It's call & response. A text to be read aloud. Sometimes there are two different dialogues occurring. I am the line between these two dialogues, mediating. Intervening.

"Everything has disappeared.
There are traces, signs. But everything has disappeared. *There are translations.*"

At times the text is shouting & whispering. Like a conversation within a conversation. As I read aloud the words waver between loud and soft. The italicized is to be whispered, just audible. The regular font is the shouting, the words you are not afraid to say. They play on each other, work together//contradict.

"La poesia se me olvida
como se me olvido tu cuerpo reventado"

The Spanish side speaks to me in ways the English translation can not. My relationship with this language resurrected, partly, through this book. There's something about reading poetry in another language. The ebb and flow off tongue in ways English fails. The forgetting of poetry. The forgetting of burst body.

I found "Intervenir/Intervene" when I was rediscovering my own story. The story of my Latinx heritage, buried with my father in 2001. I began feeling more comfortable with Spanish, making an effort to read more books in translation. Dorantes/Sanchez gave me the confidence to keep relearning, keep facing the past disappeared. Because there were traces, signs.

KNOTT'S BERRY FARM, BUENA PARK 1983

Father and me, January 1980

Grave of my paternal grandparents, 2018

I remember
as child, it
felt distant.

Mom & Dad &
me, dressed up
to affix
knees to
dirt.

Years later, familiarity.

Marble relic,
atop a hill.
Green expanse, then
downtown L.A.

He died in '85.

I was 4.

I wonder: are memories
fact or fiction?

MARTIN LUTHER KING LIBRARY,
DOWNTOWN SAN JOSE, 2018

I WENT TO THIS LIBRARY OFTEN
WHILE WRITING THE BOOK. I FOUND
SEVERAL LP'S IN THE SERIES
"TEXAS-MEXICO BORDER MUSIC."
I'D CHECK THEM OUT AND SPEND
EVENINGS LISTENING TO EACH ONE.
I MADE A MIXTAPE OF MY FAVORITE
SONGS.

//ACKNOWLEDGEMENTS

First and foremost *mucho amor a mi mamá y hermanxs*. Special thanks to my extended family for lending their histories to these words collected here, especially Tía Carmen and Tía Concha (*siempre vivirán en nuestros corazones*).

This book would not have been possible without Lynne DeSilva-Johnson and The Operating System. Thank you so much for letting me be part of the OS family.

Thank you to Li for her unwavering encouragement//support. Thank you to the lovely folx who wrote beautiful blurbs: Angel Dominguez, Lisa Donovan, and Janice Lobo Sapigao. Thanks to everyone who's eyes grazed drafts of this book and/ or who were willing to listen to me talk about this book, I appreciate you all.

Last but not least, thank you to the ashes of my father, drowned somewhere in the waters between California and Mexico.

Excerpts of this manuscript have appeared or are forthcoming online via Entropy, Pinball, and Elderly Magazine.

In 2017 a self-released zine, titled "Semillas de Tamarindo," the text of which is included here, meditated on memories contained within the preceding pages. The zine was a photocopied edition of /50.

ERICK SÁENZ is a 1st generation Latinx writer and English teacher from Los Angeles. He is founding editor of Lilac Press, a small DIY imprint. He was previously a contributing editor for the online place-based magazine *Cheers from the Wasteland*. In addition to several self-published chapbooks and zines, his work can be found at *Entropy, Alien Mouth, Elderly Magazine, Pinball, Hobart Pulp, Five:2:One magazine*, and others. *SUSURROS A MI PADRE* is his first book.

Greetings comrade! Thank you for talking to us about your process today! Can you introduce yourself, in a way that you would choose?

Hello! My name is Erick Sáenz and I am a first generation Latinx writer from Los Angeles. Self publishing is important to me because of my roots in diy//punk. I've self released two chapbooks of fiction and several zines. In addition to writing I teach high school English, follow baseball, and drink too much coffee.

Why are you a poet/writer/artist?

I've always felt comfortable with using writing as a means of self-expression. I can be a very shy person, and so finding an outlet that allows me to essentially put myself out there is important for personal growth. Writing is that for me. It's also been very therapeutic for me as I've grown older and confronted aspects of my life I ignored before.

When did you decide you were a poet/writer/artist (and/or: do you feel comfortable calling yourself a poet/writer/artist, what other titles or affiliations do you prefer/feel are more accurate)?

Historically I've been much more comfortable writing fiction. Poetry was really intimidating for a long time. It wasn't until I began experimenting with different forms outside of the school-taught curriculum that I really became comfortable with it. Recently I've gotten used to the idea of calling myself a writer, but I think teacher is the first title I think of for myself.